POETIC VOYAGES ABERDEEN

Edited by Simon Harwin

First published in Great Britain in 2001 by
YOUNG WRITERS
Remus House,
Coltsfoot Drive,
Peterborough, PE2 9JX
Telephone (01733) 890066

HB ISBN 0 75433 262 4
SB ISBN 0 75433 263 2

FOREWORD

Young Writers was established in 1991 with the aim to promote creative writing in children, to make reading and writing poetry fun.

This year once again, proved to be a tremendous success with over 88,000 entries received nationwide.

The Poetic Voyages competition has shown us the high standard of work and effort that children are capable of today. It is a reflection of the teaching skills in schools, the enthusiasm and creativity they have injected into their pupils shines clearly within this anthology.

The task of selecting poems was therefore a difficult one but nevertheless, an enjoyable experience. We hope you are as pleased with the final selection in *Poetic Voyages Aberdeen* as we are.

CONTENTS

Siobhan Wood	100
Anne Brown	101
Rebecca Thomson	102
Richard Morrison	103
Logan Neave	104
Mark Black	105
Andrea Willox	106
Lauren McKenzie	107
Hayley Fletcher	108
Callum Maclean	109
Leeza Watt	110
Lauren Reid	111
Emma McLeman	112
Samantha Harris	113
Lisa Wilson	114
Nicola Smith	115
Fraser Gulline	116
Paula Malcolm	117
Paul Gray	118
Katy Thomson	119
Greig Duncan	120
Claire Crawford	121
Craig Stephen	122
Lauren Gray	123
Alison Wylie	124
Margaret Tough	125

Maryculter West School

Callum Stewart	126
Paddy Rennie	127
Leanne Bartlett	128
Allan Green	129
Martin Scott	130
Louisa Scott	131
Lizzie Green	132
Martin Brand	133
Ali MacLeod	134
Fraser McTaggart	135

The Poems

CASTLES

Big, tall, fat castles!
Strong, stone-walled castles!
Damp, wet, miserable castles!
Bare, dull, boring castles!
Spooky, creepy, ghostly castles!
Dark, crawling, walking castles!
Murderous, dangerous, violent castles!
Still, frozen, staring castles!
Castles! Castles! Castles!

Castles!

Harriet McRae (8)
Airyhall Primary School

CASTLES!

Starless, inky, grim castles!
Gloomy, dark, haunted castles!
Huge, enormous, spooky castles!
Stone, stiff, hard castles!
Religious, old, ancient castles!
Tall, steep, mountain like castles!
Echoing, vibrating, menacing castles!
Cold, icy, chilly castles!
Castles! Castles! Castles!

Castles!

James Charleton (8)
Airyhall Primary School

CASTLES

Big, massive, large castles!
Wet, cold, damp castles!
Spooky, scary, gloomy castles!
Deathly, murderous, dangerous castles!
Horrible, dull, dark castles!
Haunted, disgusting, dirty castles!
Frozen, weeping, miserable castles!
Protective, shielding, sheltering castles!
Castles! Castles! Castles!

Castles!

Esther Gordon (8)
Airyhall Primary School

CASTLES!

Spooky, ghostly, haunted castles!
Huge, enormous, monstrous castles!
Tall, lofty, lanky castles!
Gothic, mysterious, mythic castles!
Bashful, shy, modest castles!
Skunky, sniffy, slippy castles!
Dark, dangerous, deadly castles!
Scary, unnerving, nasty castles!
Castles! Castles! Castles!

Castles!

Holly Phillips (8)
Airyhall Primary School

CASTLES!

Big, spooky, massive castles!
Old, crumbly, ancient castles!
Tall, bulky, enormous castles!
Grey, dark, dull castles!
Strong, steady, sturdy castles!
Enormous, haunted, ghostly castles!
Gigantic, monumental, voluminous castles!
Elephantine, immeasurable, large castles!
Castles! Castles! Castles!

Castles!

Andrew Gibbon (8)
Airyhall Primary School

CASTLES!

Strong, powerful, spooky castles!
Stinky, smelly, murky castles!
Huge, monstrous, gloomy castles!
Tall, stone, hard castles!
Dreadful, psychic, super castles!
Magic, dark, spooky castles,
Old, ancient, ruined castles!
Frightening, horrible, dreadful castles!
Castles! Castles! Castles!

Levi Seagraves (8)
Airyhall Primary School

CASTLE

Enormous, smelly, tall castles!
Old, grey, black castles!
Slimy, deserted, strong castles!
Tough, heavy, monstrous castles!
Muddy, colossal, bulging castles!
Ghostly, frightening, nasty castles!
Wrecked, dark, gloomy castles!
Ugly, spiky, brown castles!
Historical, cracked, massive castles!
Towering, stone, damp castles!
Castles! Castles! Castles!

Castles!

Gregor McCallan (8)
Airyhall Primary School

CASTLES!

Big, bulky, giant castles!
Wet, damp, stormy castles!
Scary, creepy, spooky castles!
Horrible, slimy, cold castles!
Dark, gloomy, dim castles!
Dangerous, deadly, violent castles!
Ghostly, horrible, haunted castles!
Protective, shielding, sheltering castles!
Castles! Castles! Castles!

Leah Fowler (8)
Airyhall Primary School

CASTLES

Leaking, wet, draughty castles!
Spooky, haunted, ghostly castles!
Bumpy, lumpy, chunky castles!
Ancient, old, crumbling castles!
Smelly, stinky, rotten castles!
Tall, strong, hard castles!
Slimy, horrible, ugly castles!
Deserted, empty, bare castles!
Castles! Castles! Castles!

Ashleigh Mair (8)
Airyhall Primary School

CASTLES!

Sturdy, tough, strong castles!
Big, bulky, colossal castles!
Soaked, drenched, slimy castles!
Dark, gloomy, spooky castles!
Brown, grey, black castles!
Dreadful, scary, crumbly castles!
Smelly, haunted, ghostly castles!
Important, serious, tall castles!
Castles! Castles! Castles!

Clark Walker (8)
Airyhall Primary School

CASTLE

Dark, dusty, gloomy castles!
Smelly, musty, rotten castles!
Big, bulky, enormous castles!
Spooky, frightening, creepy castles!
Grand, royal, posh castles!
Beautiful, pretty, stunning castles!
Solid, strong, stable castles!
Crowned, congested, overflowing castles!
Castles! Castles! Castles!

Castles!

Danielle Brown (8)
Airyhall Primary School

CASTLES

Strong, protective, big castles!
Spooky, terrifying, bad castles!
Wet, damp, dreary castles!
Violent, deadly, dangerous castles!
Ghostly, eerie, gloomy castles!
Tall, enormous, massive castles!
Turreted, dusty, dim castles!
Old, dingy, dark castles!
Castles! Castles! Castles!

Castles!

Sean Dempsey (8)
Airyhall Primary School

CASTLES

Big, large, strong castles!
Smelly, scary, spooky castles!
Freezing, cold, dreary castles!
Violent, haunted, dangerous castles!
Tall, enormous, massive castles!
Deadly, dim, dirty castles!
Mucky, old, dark castles!
Protective, towering, sheltering castles!
Castles! Castles! Castles!

Castles!

Clark Robertson (8)
Airyhall Primary School

CASTLES

Grim, dull, starless castles!
Powerful, secure, robust castles!
Immeasurable, colossal, huge castles!
Peculiar, queer, weird castles!
Ancient, antique, medieval castles!
Creepy, blood-curling, eerie castles!
Secret, mystical, magical castles!
Musky, scented, pongy castles!
Castles! Castles! Castles!

Castles!

Ross Hendry (8)
Airyhall Primary School

CASTLES

Large, dark, enormous castles!
Big, rocky, stony castles!
Black, scary, old castles!
Smelly, soaking, soggy castles!
Grey, wet, towering castles,
Slimy, watery, damp castles!
Horrible, cold, creepy castles!
Freezing, dusty, massive castles!
Castles! Castles! Castles!

Castles!

Douglas Elrick (8)
Airyhall Primary School

CASTLES

Big, bulky, colossal castles!
Murky, dim, sombre castles!
Murderous, ruthless, savage castles!
Strong, defensive, shielding castles!
Grimy, dirty, dusty castles!
Tall, towering, lofty castles!
Silent, quiet, muffled castles!
Whispering, murmuring, undertone castles!
Castles! Castles! Castles!

Castles!

Oliver McIntosh-Prentice (8)
Airyhall Primary School

CASTLES

Spooky, creepy, scary castles!
Tall, high, lofty castles!
Haunted, ghostly, spooky castles!
Grey, dark, dull castles!
Strong, tough, sturdy castles!
Old, ancient, historic castles!
Big, enormous, huge castles!
Damp, wet, slippy castles!
Castles! Castles! Castles!

Castles!

Michael Stec (8)
Airyhall Primary School

CASTLES

Spooky, scary, haunted castles!
Deadly, dangerous, nasty castles!
Cold, dark, dripping castles!
Wet, horrible, sloppy castles!
Rotten, killing, stone castles!
Big, huge, jumbo castles!
Smelly, stinky, horrid castles!
Hard, solid, rock castles!

Ross Thom (8)
Airyhall Primary School

CASTLES

Big, enormous, massive castles!
Wet, damp, dripping castles!
Dusty, sandy, crumbly castles!
Muddy, messy, dirty castles!
Gloomy, dark, murky castles!
Heavy, bulky, large castles!
Haunted, spooky, ghostly castles!
Grey, horrible, wet castles!
Big, strong, stony castles!
Castles! Castles! Castles!

Castles!

Christopher Brooks (8)
Airyhall Primary School

AUTUMN - I DON'T WANT TO DIE

Autumn is a sad sailor.
Scared sailor.
Tired from pulling in the net
Miserable, getting wet,
He's clumsy as the boat rocks to and fro,
He is whistling,
He is crying for home,
He is mumbling.
The boat is creaking.
He thinks of when he was young.
Sad, scared, sailor.

Ryan Lawrence (10)
Balmedie Primary School

BAD MOODS

Black as night, bang into red,
The red is like hell but worse,
The tastes of hot pepper,
Are melting in my throat,
The smell of melting plastic
And flames are in the air,
Bombs are blowing up,
There is a never stopping shout of terror,
Balls of fire hitting everyone,
Makes my body melt with rage,
When I am in a mood.

Craig Bruce (10)
Balmedie Primary School

IS IT THE GROUND?

How did I get here?
Why was it me?
Among the chirping howling sounds?
All I see is rays of light,
All I hear is bouncing signals.

Oh how? Oh how did I get here?
Oh why was it me?
Among the rattling jars and echoes,
All I see is bubbles of green,
All I hear is giggling.

Oh why was it me?
And how did I get here?
Among the crispy white rain,
All I hear is my heartbeat,
All I feel is the ground.

It wasn't the ground,
It was a sound,
A ray of sound,
Clashing,
Falling,
Falling,
Falling,
Thump,
This is the ground.

Josephine Morland (10)
Balmedie Primary School

AUTUMN

Autumn is
A soldier in pain,
A soldier that's sad,
A soldier that's tired,
A soldier shaking with fear,
A soldier running as fast as he can,
A soldier shooting his enemy,
The soldier is moaning,
The soldier is thinking of what he would be doing with his family.
He is thinking of the happiest time with his family.

Graeme Stuart (10)
Balmedie Primary School

SLEEPING ANGER

Anger is the sound of burning,
Twisting, tossing and even turning,
Smoke and fire everywhere,
It's just so hard to even bear,
Another planet somewhere,
With lots of people and fresh air.

Billy Coupar (10)
Balmedie Primary School

THE POEM ABOUT THE ATMOSPHERE

Why am I here?
Looking at the burning, orange sun,
In the bright, blue sky.
I look down, frightened of falling,
I always hear three clocks chiming every hour.
Why is it me all the time?
I see a silver rollercoaster swirling round and round.
Hearing faint violins playing.
I look around at plants singing and moving,
I look above listen to the birds tweeting,
Goods sounds sifting.
Bad sounds escaping,
It is time to go back to Earth.

Paula Buchan (10)
Balmedie Primary School

LIFE IS A BORE

Danielle Brands!
First alarm of the morning,
'What' was the answer,
'You're going to be late for school,
Now tidy your room, it looks like a pig sty.'
'I will, I will.'
'Now brush your hair, it looks like a dog's dinner,'
Later in the car, ready for school.
'Danielle stop fighting with your brother,
It sounds like an elephant parade back there.'
Mum's voice goes in one ear and out the other.
'Be quiet, I'm trying to drive,
I'm going to crash any minute.'
At school it doesn't improve.
'I don't see that pencil moving Danielle,'
At the same time,
'I don't see smoke coming out that pencil Danielle,'
The teacher's voice never stops,
'Nag, nag, nag!'
All day long,
Life is a bore.

Danielle Brands (11)
Balmedie Primary School

ANGER IN THE MORNING

Anger in the morning, starting with breakfast,
I have homework to finish,
I'm tired,
I'm bored,
Before breakfast I rolled out of bed and hit my head!
I'm grumpy,
I'm grunting,
My head is red about to explode.
I've got a taste of red-hot peppers,
I'm hungry,
I'm annoyed,
I have the smell of fire burning,
I have the look of a house on fire,
I'm sulking,
I'm shouting,
In my head, I have the sounds of drums banging loudly,
I won't be happy for the rest of the day.
I'm huffing,
I'm puffing,
That's me in a mood.

Malcolm MacDonald (10)
Balmedie Primary School

ATMOSPHERE DISASTER

Why does it have to be me?
Listening to wind whistling,
Comets going by,
UFO's lights flashing in the dark,
Solar max exploding,
Fumes swirling and floating,
Volcanoes are erupting,
Roller coaster's rolling,
Am I going to die?
Can I get home?
Scared of floating away into outer space on my own.

Sandy MacDonald (10)
Balmedie Primary School

THE ATMOSPHERE

Why did it have to be me?
Floating ten thousand miles above my Earth.
Listening to bells chiming, stings pinging,
Comets shooting past,
Stars gleaming in the dark.
Planets spin round and round,
Where could I be?
Fumes and gases floating up,
Closer and closer they come,
Where are they coming from?
The o-zone layer breaks,
Down shoots the sun's rays,
Earth has come to an end.

Lyam Walburn (10)
Balmedie Primary School

DARK

Grey as a dark, dark man in his coat,
Tastes as a brown sauce in my throat,
Smells of bleach in the sink.
Feeling lost in a twister - sounds like
I want to run away.
The weatherman drives me crazy.
Homework!
Ahh! My brother.
I go and cry in my room,
Stamping up the stairs,
Slamming the door,
My teeth closing together.

Connie Reid (10)
Balmedie Primary School

BAD MOODS

My sister is annoying me,
I feel like I'm going to explode,
I'm tasting hot spicy pepper,
I hear the church choir singing in my ears,
I see orange fire burning,
Loud noises, bang, bang, bang
Are surrounding me.
Silver robots coming,
Cars are speeding,
Ghosts are yelling,
Red lava flowing,
Yellow lightning is striking,
I hate my bad mood!

Jennifer Heritage (10)
Balmedie Primary School

NAGGING

My mum's been nagging me all day,
Nag, nag, nag is her way,
Your room's a mess,
Why don't you get dressed?
Brush your teeth, then wash your face,
Have some Frosties,
Call your mate,
Don't be late,
Get on the bus,
Without any fuss.

Into school,
'Why are you late?'
'We missed the bus so my mum made a fuss.'
Line up for assembly in a long line,
'Be quiet, how old are you now? You must be just over nine!
You should know better, you should know fine,
Beep, beep, beep, beep, who's watch is that?
Where is it at?
Switch it off, that little clock,
Shhh do not talk,
Back in the class,
We'll do some maths.'
Time to go home,
So I'm finishing this poem!

Meghan Leith (10)
Balmedie Primary School

MOONBEAMS

The moonbeams through my window,
Its gentle aura of what seems blue,
Calming,
Shining silver upon the sea,
Bright, lunar light,
I feel so content,
As it orbits the gem,
Our planet Earth.

Kerry McLaughlin (10)
Balmedie Primary School

BAD MOODS

Red bad moods like a fire,
A forest before my eyes.
Rubber burning with salt,
Chilli pepper inside my mouth.
I smell onion and garlic, all yuck,
Makes me feel sick.
I see a graveyard at night,
A storm coming over it.
I hear the storm outside,
I hear the opera singer scream,
I need out,
Help, help
Madness!

Kirsteen Stevenson (10)
Balmedie Primary School

BAD MOODS

Bad moods are as black as the night sky,
The sun and moon are not out,
Bad moods taste like hot chilli deep down in
My throat burning away my tonsils,
Bad moods smell like burning fire
With lots of smoke.
Bad moods look like a volcano erupting,
I'm in the middle,
Bad moods sound like someone scratching
A blackboard.
Screeching in my ears,
Bad moods feel like something burning
Deep down in my stomach.

Kieran Morrison (10)
Balmedie Primary School

A LIMERICK

There once was a lady called Ann
Who lived in an old caravan.
She ate bubble and squeak
And a carrot and leek
And married a little old man.

Gemma Armstrong (10)
Balmedie Primary School

NAG, NAG, NAG

'You're driving me up the wall,
You've lost your marbles,
Are you a tortoise?'

That's my mum nagging me in the morning.

'I want to see smoke coming from your pencil,
Less talking, more thinking,
If you fall and crack your head, it's not my fault.'

That's my teacher nagging me at school
'Other people know it's raining too Adam.'
'It's not fair,'
'It goes in one ear and out the other.'
That's my friends nagging me in the playground.

'Your teeth are as yellow as the sun,
I'm surprised you haven't got square eyes yet,
Adam your breath stinks,'
That's my family nagging me in the evening.

Adam Copp (10)
Balmedie Primary School

SNOWY WEATHER

The snow white, snow whirls softly down,
Snowflakes through the air,
Children have a great time
Playing on the snow,
Robins singing,
People slipping on the ice.
Robin can't find food,
People giving children drifters,
Mums and dads shuffling the snow,
Helping old people across the street.

Snowflake falling on the ground,
Nobody likes getting snow kicked at them,
Over the street there is ice and somebody could fall,
No breathe of wind and rain,
Making it slipping for children,
Children keep warm in the winter.

Danielle Donald
Bramble Brae Primary School

SNOWY WEATHER

The soft white snow swirls softly down,
It lands on the icy ground,
Children playing in the snow,
Making lovely angels.
Out playing snowball fights.
Making big slides,
Hedgehogs are lucky, they are hibernating,
Mums and dads are shovelling some away from paths,
While we're out having fun,
Robins sing as we play,
Cars are being abandoned.
Powdery flakes fall on your head,
Or if you go outside you get a surprise.
Snow is drifting as we move,
All dressed up warmly.
Helping old people cross the road.
As you breath, the air comes out all white.
Every night is getting dark and cold,
Snowploughs clear the roads.
You can sit inside by the fire,
Keep nice and warm until the next
Snowy, stormy day comes.

Kara Anne Paton
Bramble Brae Primary School

SNOWY WEATHER

The soft, white snow whirls softly down,
Snowflakes twirling in the sky.
Softly down comes the snow,
Robins sing in the trees,
Making slides on every hill,
Mums and dads clearing the icy paths,
A white blanket covers the garden.

Dawn Mair (11)
Bramble Brae Primary School

SNOWY WEATHER

The soft, white snow whirls softly down,
The ground is white covered in snow,
Most children go out on their sledges,
Clear the paths before you slip.
Watching the snow fall, it is bright and white,
Making snowmen, getting cold,
Robins cannot find food,
Snow starts to change to ice,
Start sliding, having fun,
Snow is drifting on the ground,
There is no breathe of wind,
School's closed, staying outside,
Robin sings, no wind.

Cara Paterson (11)
Bramble Brae Primary School

SNOWY WEATHER

The soft white snow whirls softly down,
Children ice-skating on frozen ponds,
Ice ploughs cleaning paths and roads,
Flakes of snow falling and patting you on the head.
Cars covered in snow,
Still and quiet,
No more school for a week,
Bobsleigher's having fun,
Sledges and huskies all over town,
Coal fires, warm,
Electricity has run out.
Robin singing to keep him contented,
Cars stranded and white,
Red car has turned white overnight,
Happy kids making snow angels.

Jade Park (11)
Bramble Brae Primary School

SNOWY WEATHER

The soft white snow whirls softly down,
Door's getting blocked by snow.
Cars crashing because of the ice,
Ice on your windows,
All of the cars abandoned.
All of the plants dying down,
Everything frozen,
When the snow goes away and everyone is sad,
Children skating on the ponds
And ice is going away,
Rabbits are frozen and dying.

Marcus Paton
Bramble Brae Primary School

SNOWY WEATHER

The soft white snow whirls softly down,
Old ladies warm up by the fire,
Snowballs fly everywhere,
Snowmen in every garden,
Engines crack in the ice,
Powdery flakes fall everywhere,
Snowploughs busy every day,
Kids clearing paths for their mums,
No one sings like a robin,
A snowstorm happens every day,
Abandoned cars always jutting out of the snow.

Wayne McDermid (11)
Bramble Brae Primary School

SNOWY WEATHER

The soft white snow whirls down,
People getting drifters in the snow,
Jumping off fences into deep, soft snow,
Building two part snowmen in schools,
Lots of accidents happening on the roads,
Abandoned cars left to rot,
People slipping on thin ice
And braking one of their bones,
Squirrels gather nuts to last them
Until the snow goes away,
Snowploughs cleaning the road
For the drivers going to work.
Robin's sad because the berries are
Covered with white snow,
Homeless people needing shelter and food.

Daniel Courtley
Bramble Brae Primary School

SNOWY WEATHER

The soft, white snow whirls softly down
Snowdrifts along the roads,
Leaves flutter in the air like butterflies,
Owls howl among the hills,
Frosty white grass,
Children sledging and having fun,
The wind whispers quietly,
Birds hide from coldness,
Children laugh in the snow.
Wet clothes waiting to be dried,
Snowflakes circulating everywhere,
Hedgehogs hibernating,
Tractors cleaning roads,
Making slides,
Very dark nights,
Snowmen all around,
Farmers out early,
Cold, frosty days.
The snow whistling like never before,
People wrapped up warm,
The ground covered in snow,
Footprints making patterns.

Stacey Morrison (11)
Bramble Brae Primary School

SNOWY WEATHER

The soft white snow whirls softly down,
Snow makes cars have accidents,
Children having fun having snowball fights,
Snowploughs having fun, pushing snow to the side.
Sledging down hills.
Cats want in and want to stay warm,
'Hot cup of tea' I shout,
Friends push you over and give you a drifter,
Can't get out, too cold and get bored.

Richie Ross
Bramble Brae Primary School

IT WAS A WONDERFUL DAY

Goodbye wonderful day,
This day has been the best day,
The sun has been shining.

The stars are waiting,
For the sun to move on,
The moon will be out soon.

It's so dark,
I can't see my hands,
My head is nipping.

I can't stand it,
I hate the moonlight,
I wish it would just leave me.

I was well in the afternoon,
But now is the worst time of the day,
I hate night-time, I hate night-time.

I just can't wait until tomorrow.

10 o'clock, time for bed,
10 o'clock, time for bed.

It was a wonderful day.

Sean Strachan (11)
Bucksburn Primary School

Night-Time

In the night, the owl's hoot,
At the same time, cars show their headlights,
The moon shining bright in the window,
Strange noises made from the crickets,
Tick-tock, the clock hits ten.

The water tapping from the tap,
The wind blowing litter about,
Stars shining in the night,
Tick-tock, the clock hits eleven.

Birds flying in the night,
Lights are flickering out in the night,
Cats screeching in the garden,
Tick-tock, the clock hits twelve.

James Buthlay (12)
Bucksburn Primary School

NIGHT-TIME

'It's so late at night.'

As the people drink the pubs dry,
You hear the dog amplifying its cry.
Foxes going through the trash,
Banks beware, thieves are after your cash.

'It's so late at night.'

Thank you for the end of another day,
It has been much fun.
Not to long to go now,
Before the start of another one.

Calum Spence (11)
Bucksburn Primary School

LATE AT NIGHT

It's so late at night,
The moonlight shining outside,
The cars on the road go beep, beep,
It's so late at night.
The party next door goes thump,
The little stars outside twinkle,
This is just to say goodnight,
It's so late at night.

Joanne Cramond (11)
Bucksburn Primary School

LATE AT NIGHT

It is so late at night,
I can hear some mice,
Rushing on the kitchen floor
Tip, tap goes the little feet,
Tick-tock goes the big grandfather clock.

Then it strikes twelve o'clock
I must have been hearing things,
I heard a ghost go *boo*
But it was just my son
Crying at his door.

But then I heard the doorbell
Go ding dong
I got out of bed
Who would it be?
It was only my husband.

Steven Sinclair (11)
Bucksburn Primary School

NIGHT-TIME

This is just to say thank you
For the gleam of the moon,
Like a torch in the sky,
The chug, chug, chug of the cars going by,
Music from parties that last all night long,
People coming home from the long day,
This is just to say thank you.

Chris Mair (12)
Bucksburn Primary School

IT WAS A WONDERFUL DAY

Goodbye day

You have pleased me
   from morning till night
      all day, every day
         You have pleased me.

The moon is popping out
   and the sun is disappearing
      the day has been wonderful
         nothing has gone wrong.

Following the tick
   of my clock
      it's nearly nine o'clock
      and the stars have come out.

      Nine o'clock time for bed
      Nine o'clock time for bed
      I'm in my bed
      For a while
      For a while

      Goodbye day.

Nicky Freeland (11)
Bucksburn Primary School

NIGHT-TIME

This is just to say thank you

To the sound of the clock in the cupboard
like a rooster
on a hillside.

To the cars and train
rolling past
like the clatter
of a thousand pans.

To the sound of the fishtank filter
humming all night long
like a prison guard
patrolling the corridors.

Seven o'clock, time to get up
Seven o'clock, time to get up

The night's been going on
for so long
for so long

This is just to say thank you.

Mark Curry (11)
Bucksburn Primary School

NIGHT'S BRINGING

It's so late at night.

> As the birds go to sleep,
> No words spoken not even
> A cheep, cheep.

It's so late at night.

> Alcohol, parties, party poppers,
> But no sign of teeny boppers.

It's so late at night.

> Everyone is sleeping tight,
> To all a goodnight.

It's so late at night.

Danielle Bavidge (11)
Bucksburn Primary School

WHEN I GROW UP

When I grow up
I want to be a secret agent
And have a gun
But I hope, it will be fun.
Now it's getting harder
Because the worst mission is yet to come.

The hot lava is scary
And the lions are hairy,
The lava was too hot so I
Got burnt on the spot.

Cameron Allan (8)
Ferryhill Primary School

WHEN I GROW UP

When I grow up
I would like to do
People's hair, make it
All nice and spiky.

I would dye people's hair
Pink, purple and yellow,
If they like green or
Blue, I would put their hair in a bun.

Or in curly curlers and
In purple plaits, I would
Like to be a hairdresser
Like my aunty.

Sammy Scott (8)
Ferryhill Primary School

WHEN I GROW UP

When I grow up, I want to be a spaceman
And fly like an eagle but a lot higher and
Fly through the stars and visit Mars.

I think it would be fun to go to Jupiter
And everything to float in the air.

Kyle McQueen (9)
Ferryhill Primary School

WHEN I GROW UP

When I grow up
I'd like to be a rugby player
But rugby is very tough.

My mum is sitting in the stand
And I am playing on the pitch
And I like to play at left wing
And score 800 tries.

I would enjoy being a rugby player
And score lots of penalty goals
But on my first game I played -
We won 89-88.

Rugby is a good game to play
The second time I played
A match we lost 38-17.

Kyle Paterson (9)
Ferryhill Primary School

WHEN I GROW UP

When I grow up
I want to be a football player,
To get some money,
I would like to play for Aberdeen,
I would like to be number ten.

After a match, I would have a bath,
Then I would ask my manager,
When the match will be on TV,
He says 'tomorrow'
Then I'd go home and have my tea.

Bruce Smith (8)
Ferryhill Primary School

WHEN I GROW UP

When I grow up
I would like to be a clown
I'd have a million dollars
And my very own crown.

I'd turn a mouse into a house
And turn a goat into a boat
And sail it all the way
I'll turn you into whatever you say.

I'd make people happy
I might get some 'boos'
But who really cares
I've got nothing to lose.

Kieran Heads (8)
Ferryhill Primary School

WHEN I GROW UP

When I grow up
I'd like to be a dancer,
Dancing in lots of
Different places.

I will wear a
Sparkly dress and
Sparkly shoes, dancing
All day and all night.

People taking pictures and
Cheering for me
I am very, very
Happy you see.

Sarah Mark (9)
Ferryhill Primary School

WHEN I GROW UP

When I grow up
I would like to be
A knight, big and bold
With a great big sword.

I would kill a dragon
And get all the gold
I would live in a castle
And have a great big army.

I would kill the Duke of Edinburgh
And defeat the Royal Navy
Step by step I would become famous.

Stuart Gill (8)
Ferryhill Primary School

WHEN I GROW UP

When I grow up
I would like to be a doctor
So I could learn about the body
And earn a lot of money!

It would be interesting to see
What it looked like inside you.

I would make everyone that
Came to me feel better in
No time.

Calum McIlraith (9)
Ferryhill Primary School

WHEN I GROW UP

When I grow up,
When I grow up,
I want to be an astronaut,
I would fly in my space ship,
Round and round and round.

I would land on the moon
And have some cheese.

I would go back to
Earth and bring a bright
Moon stone back to Earth.

Lewis Masson (9)
Ferryhill Primary School

WHEN I GROW UP

When I grow up
I would like to be
A football player
And score a lot of goals.

I would play for Manchester United
And be up front with Beckham.

I will be a multi-millionaire
And maybe rule the world
And I'll play against Dundee United
And win 5-3.

Jamie Noble
Ferryhill Primary School

WHEN I GROW UP

When I grow up
I'll be a doctor
I could help grannies
With high blood pressure.

At midday
It's very busy
And when I get home
I will be dizzy.

The next day
It was not busy
I was very bored
Not doing anything at all.

I was just reading a newspaper
Then I heard the door
People came in
And I got more money.

After helping all the patients
I was tired
In my snooze, I heard a voice saying
'You're fired!'

Rory Innes (9)
Ferryhill Primary School

WHEN I GROW UP

I'd like to be a singer
Standing on the stage
With a sparkly dress and high heel shoes,
Smiling all the way.

The audience would cheer at me
When I come out on stage
I would sing like a nightingale
And I don't know how much I'm paid.

If I became a singer, I wouldn't want to stop,
Because I know that I'm the best
Out of the whole lot
A singer is all I ever want to be.

Sophie Hamill (9)
Ferryhill Primary School

WHEN I GROW UP

When I grow up
I would like to be a policeman
I would fight
Solve mysteries,
Might even chase them down town.

I would maybe have to whack them
For the right,
I would dive on the crook's cat
And arrest them for sure.

I would go in the crook's house
And get the gold and return it
To its original home.

John Callender (9)
Ferryhill Primary School

WHEN I GROW UP

When I grow up
I'd like to be a model
Walking down the stage
With a pretty dress and a smile on my face.

Cameras flashing, people watching,
Makes me nervous a lot,
Trying on new clothes,
I've never seen before.

I've even seen myself in magazines
And in the paper too,
My hair is all shiny
And smells of nice shampoo.

Holly Webster (8)
Ferryhill Primary School

WHEN I GROW UP

When I grow up
I want to be an astronaut
And go up into space
But that's a big thing to face.

Me in my small rocket
And Christopher that's all,
We'll go through stars
And visit Mars.

Laughing all the way
And have a drink at the Milky Way,
Then we'll go past the galaxy
And visit a planet far beyond and Chris
Says he wants a magic wand.

Just then I notice something wrong
Oh no the fuel's gone!
Then we crash on an unknown planet,
But then we see an alien's shop.

But we have no alien cash
Then someone calls my name
Then I wake up
And the teacher's not amused.

But I don't mind
Even though I'm behind with my work.

Moe Keir (9)
Ferryhill Primary School

WHEN I GROW UP

I'd like to be a football player
Score goals every day,
I wouldn't like to stop
Because I'll stop getting paid.

I will play a game of footy,
With my friends all day
Cause I will get great practise
For the big game.

Joe Innes (9)
Ferryhill Primary School

WHEN I GROW UP

When I grow up
I want to be a spaceman
To fly to Mars
To fly to space
And come back home through space.

I talked to an alien
Through space and came back down
And went away.

Calum Nicol (8)
Ferryhill Primary School

WHEN I GROW UP

When I grow up
I would like to be a nurse
So I could help all the patients
When they're ill.

But soon they will not be ill
I would send them home without a pill
And hopefully I would not see them again.

Erin Fyfe (8)
Ferryhill Primary School

WHEN I GROW UP

When I grow up
I want to be
A skater dancing round
With the music
What a sound!

I'm going to wear a dress
All sparkling with jewels
I've seen skaters on the TV
And heard them on the news.

My boots are all nice and white,
My hair is up with glitter in it too
And I'm getting all excited behind the silky curtains
Then I go out and do my show
Now I'm not nervous any more.

Alice Milne (8)
Ferryhill Primary School

WHEN I GROW UP

I want to be
A hairdresser going snip, snap,
Cutting hair is so much fun.

Putting hair in a bun,
In a bun is very good fun,
I put colour in men's hair,
That's the ones that aren't bald
And I get a lot of money.

Emily McDonald (9)
Ferryhill Primary School

WHEN I GROW UP

When I grow up
I would like to be an astronaut
And fly up into space
And I think it would be absolutely ace.

I would pass Mars and Jupiter
And maybe even Saturn
I'm glad I am with my friend Moe
Because we are heading for the sun
Well at least I'm eating a lovely Chinese bun.

We landed on Uranus,
Where we met a alien called Aranus
Who was very, very kind
So we went to his master called Mister, Mister Pride.

We took pictures of everything
And headed back to Earth
And now I get £200,000 every month.

Christopher Moore (9)
Ferryhill Primary School

When I Grow Up

When I grow up
I would like to be a vet
And treat animals
And get money all day.

If Sophie's cat gets hurt
I'll treat it straight away
An animal has come in, oh no,
It's my turn to operate on it.

Gems Johnson (8)
Ferryhill Primary School

PLAYGROUND WEATHER

When I hear the bell
It feels like I am falling
Down a well.
When teachers
Are in the staff-room,
They are nice and warm.

When we are in the playground,
I start to freeze.
When the playground is hot,
It is better but surely gets wetter,
Sometimes it is windy and stormy
But it is best when I come to school
And the sky is light blue.

Paul Gibb (8)
Ferryhill Primary School

RED NOSE DAY

Red Nose Day
Red Nose Day
It's a laugh
With presenters and competitions
It will be a blast.

Comic Relief
Will do a fund
To give kids
The chance to have fun
And get a better life.

Jonathon Milne (10)
Gilcomstoun Primary School

LET'S GO OUT

Come, come, come on. Let's go out.
Mum says it's cold but dad says it's not.
But I see it is sure fine outside. So let's go
Out as soon as possible.

Me and Dad dragged Mum outside to the park.
Dad got some ice creams.

Then we went to the park,
Then we went home.
Mum went upstairs
She screamed so loud,
The whole house can hear my mum
But Mum fainted.

Shazida Begum (10)
Gilcomstoun Primary School

IF ONLY

If only I were thin, then I would win every pageant
I was in - I wouldn't be embarrassed at gym
If only I was thin.

If only I could control my anger, then I wouldn't
Feel sadder when arguing,
If only I could control my anger.

If only I was smarter, then it wouldn't matter
If I lost a test,
If only I was smarter.

If only I had more friends, then I wouldn't have to pretend I do
If only I had more friends.

If only it wasn't me who gets bullied, then
I wouldn't be so tense
If only it wasn't me.

If only Mum had a better job, then I wouldn't
Have to sob when we run out of money
If only Mum had a better job.

If only life wasn't stoney like a road,
If only, if only.

Ayesha Ibrahim (11)
Gilcomstoun Primary School

ONE DARK, COLD NIGHT

It's night, it's night and you are there,
Out in the dark, it's just not fair.
In the cold, dark streets, you wander around,
Thinking about what you just might meet
Which would try and kill you.

A yeti, a goblin, a bigfoot too,
It doesn't matter, it's only you,
If they see you they won't even dare,
Especially if you move your hair,
I know it's not really fair
But no one seems to really care.

It's cold, it's cold, it's very cold
And you are not wearing a glove or even a pair,
You need a hat or maybe a coat,
Especially to cover that hair.

Remember, remember to keep out of sight,
Of the witch that rides every night,
With her cat at the back and her
Wand in her hand, you never know
It might rain sand.

It's nearly dawn and you are in
Trying to get a bed at the inn,
You get one but in the end,
You find it's full of creepy slimes.

Samantha Thompson (10)
Gilcomstoun Primary School

FLUFFY

I have a pet named Fluffy
If I take her out the cage,
My sister goes all huffy,
Till one morning I woke up and she wasn't there.
I thought to tell my sister
But then I thought I shouldn't dare
And then I searched everywhere,
I still couldn't find her, not even a hair,
I thought to myself what should I do?
If my sister finds out she will go cuckoo.
I had another check to see if the hamster was around,
But I couldn't see her a lot, not even a sound.
I looked around again, I eventually found her,
I put her back in the cage and she started to rage
I calmed her down,
Then I heard not even a sound.

Richard Robert Pitcairn (10)
Gilcomstoun Primary School

THE DIGI POEM

It was on a Friday
I remember it well
There was a black hole in the sky
Little things fell from the sky
Where the hole hid.
The things were cute
They said were called Digimon
Then some more came
But they were twenty times bigger than me
But lucky for me
The grew bigger
They said they were away to Digivolve
They beat that evil Digimon
They told me their names
I forgot them in a second
We went inside my house
I showed them my Game Boy
They were scared of it
They said they came from the Digiworld
We saw another monster
His name was Devimon
Everyone Digivolved
They beat him
Then they left.

Stuart Berry (10)
Gilcomstoun Primary School

LET'S GO SHOPPING

Grab a trolley! Let's go!
Push the trolley round and round
Dash up and down the lanes
But watch out, someone might complain.
Grab some food, make sure you get the peas and cheese
And dash down the aisle for the mince for tea
And don't forget the strawberry jelly please!
Now speed down to the juice
Watch out, don't shove or push,
Get to the cola and orange and grab some of that
Remember to get the porridge
Oh! Get some of the fruit
And don't forget the tomato soup!
Now go to the vegetables, get some carrots and potatoes
Look over there, our next door neighbour's talking like parrots.
Now let's get the organic food cause I'm in the mood,
Now let's go to the till to pay our bill!

Natalie Black (10)
Gilcomstoun Primary School

MOONLIGHT

The night light is the moonlight
Tonight I promise you my dear,
Tonight in the moonlight you have nothing to fear.
Let me sweep you off your feet tonight,
We will rise up to the clouds on a ray of moonlight.
Tonight as you wait in your tower
Hour after hour I will come on a ray of light,
Tonight, tonight, tonight, tonight.

I love the way the moonlight shines in your hair,
Tonight, tonight my dear let yourself know,
In my world of moonlight, you have nothing to fear,
You know I will treat you right,
In my world of moonlight.
The stars glitter in your eyes
My heart cries because you keep leaving
At the first light of dawn.
I wish you not to marry a mortal,
Or else my love will close forever.
So my dear lady please
Or you may have something to fear.

Kathryn Victoria Reid (10)
Gilcomstoun Primary School

ONE EARLY MORNING

Woke up one early morning in my bed,
Went down the stairs,
Saw some smoke,
My toast was burning,
My sausages were on fire.

Went to school that early morning,
Didn't know that I still had on my PJ's,
Went back home, got on my clothes
And went back to school,
When my teacher was just coming in.

Went in the class, when there was a fight,
I got a smack on the nose,
Then Joe got punched on the lip,
Then we stopped when the head teacher was standing there,
Then we went down to his office.

Went back to class,
Then got on with our work,
Then the bell went,
So we got our lunch
And went outside.

We played football,
Then the ball got kicked over the wall,
So we ran out of school and got it,
We got back in,
Luckily no one had seen us.

Then the bell went, so we went inside,
We went in the class,
We worked so hard,
That time flew by
That the home bell went.

Jamie Andrew Grieve (10)
Gilcomstoun Primary School

MAGICAL MUSIC

Magical music is in the air,
Magical music is everywhere.
If you stop, have a look around,
Some magical music is sure to be found,
Listen to the wind through the trees,
Listen to the buzz of the bees,
Listen to the tick in your clock,
Listen to your feet when you walk.

Crotchets and quavers are some types of beats,
But don't worry they are not the ones that you eat.
Slurs and ties are really cool,
But they are not the ones that you wear to school,

When I listen to music, I tap my feet,
To that really funky beat,
I nod my head as it goes along
I also sometimes sing the song,
When at night I go to bed,
Thoughts go running through my head,
Of different music that I've heard,
Some as gentle as a bird.

Music I think is such a great thing
Happiness is what it brings,
My poem has now come to an end
I hope that you liked it, my friend.

Amanda Montague (11)
Glashieburn Primary School

FOOTBALL

I like football
It is lots of fun
I also like to play it,
In the shining sun.

I like football,
It is very rough,
If you want to play it,
You have to be tough.

I like football,
It is great,
Especially when playing with my mate.

I like football,
It is the best
And it is better than the rest.

I like football,
When I score
Then my fans shout
            More!
                    More!
                            More!

Peter McLaughlan (11)
Glashieburn Primary School

ANIMALS

Animals I really like
But sometimes they like to bite
I think dogs are the best
They are better than the rest
Dogs are cute, when they go to play
I could pat them every day.

I really like rabbits
And I think it's cute that they like carrots,
I like it when they hop about the hutch,
Which makes me like them just as much,
One of my rabbits is called Tyson,
But 'Phew' I'm glad I don't have a bison.

I also like bulldogs, they are very cool
Except I don't like it when they drool,
They are also very greedy
But also can be very speedy,
Not like a very slow snail,
But the annoying thing is their whippy tail.

Hamsters are very, very small,
I think it's sweet when they run in their ball,
I think it's cute when they come to play
Except they come out at night, not the day.

Now I have come to the end of my poem,
I hope you didn't find it incredibly boring.

Lindsay Jackson (11)
Glashieburn Primary School

SEASONS

Summer is the very best time
When the sun should always shine
Children are shading,
Away from the sun
While adults bask in the sun.

Spring is here at last
Snowdrops and daffodils are vast
Children picking as they pass
While the lambs are jumping fast.

In autumn it's changing time
The skies are dark,
The leaves fill the parks,
Birds fly south to find the sun
While we stay here with none.

Icy snowflakes come tumbling down
They make people moan and frown
But when they see the fields of snow
They grab a sledge and off they go!

Leah Dargie (11)
Glashieburn Primary School

PUSSY CATS

Pussy cats sit on a cold wall,
Watching people playing with a colourful ball,
Pussy cats playing with flowers which are tall,
They play with shoe laces, pens and they do
Lots of funny things,
They pounce and jump over things,
Pussy cats sleep when they are really tired,
Some big, some small, some chubby, some thin.

Pussy cats are fun to watch
Some cats can climb up trees
But others just fall down.

There are all different colours of cats,
Brown, black, grey and lots, lots more,
Pussy cats are my favourite pets,
I've got a cat and she hates the vets,
Her name is Truffles and she eats and eats,
When she races with other cats, she cheats.

Cats see in the dark,
But they don't like it when dogs bark,
Cats run after mice
But I don't think it's nice.

Nicola Bailey (11)
Glashieburn Primary School

BUTTERFLIES

Butterflies have bright coloured wings,
They fly about with the birds that sing.
They have pretty colours like pink, purple and blue,
Butterflies fly around and birds fly too.
Butterflies flap their wings to fly
If one goes in your eye, it might make you cry.
Butterflies sit on a petal,
If you make tea, it might sit on your kettle.

Butterflies are a beautiful sight,
They only come out when it's light.
The butterflies might come out all through the year
But dads better watch that they don't fall in their beers.
Butterflies are as light as a feather,
Nothing like a piece of leather,
Butterflies fly up very high,
But they must be careful in case they die.

Hollie Brown (11)
Glashieburn Primary School

THE STRANGE PLANETS

Mercury is a planet made from fur,
But it does not purr,
It is quite big
And it wears a wig.
Venus is cool,
But it is a fool,
Watch out it might make you go in a pool.
Earth has lots of water but not of land,
Steps are my favourite band,
It spins around on one hand,
Mars is made out of Mars bars,
But not cars,
I wish it was made of melted chocolate,
Then I would eat it bit by bit.
Jupiter has a red dot,
It is the size of a pot.
There is only one dot not a lot.
Saturn has a few rings,
Which ping,
Round and round, then they ding.
Uranus is very chilly,
It is very silly,
No it does not have any lilies.
Neptune makes a lovely sound,
It sometimes goes to the bank to get a pound,
No it does not go to the dog pound.
Pluto goes to the dancing club,
But not the pub,
In netball it's a sub.

Laura Napier (11)
Glashieburn Primary School

PARENTS' NIGHT

Today is parents' night
My mum and dad are going
What am I going to do? That's right,
I'll just go out and play bowling.

I think I might have failed maths,
I might be OK in language,
I think I might be OK even
In doing a first aid bandage.

My teacher Miss Smith can never ever miss
A glance or a whisper or two
She's shouting
And never catches a glance of me or you.

I just hope I get a good report
To please my mum and dad
Then I'll get that thing I've always wanted
Those nice little bike knee pads.

I hear the car stop outside,
I run to hide in my bed,
I hear my mum and dad come up
5, 4, 3, 2, 1 I wish I was dead.

Amina Ahmed (11)
Glashieburn Primary School

THE ALIENS ARE HERE TO STAY

In the middle of the night,
Came a beam of light,
That came from the sky
And caught my eye.

The light in the sky
That caught my eye,
Were big spaceships,
With legs that kick.

I thought what kind of place,
Was it like in space,
Then I was beamed up,
In some kind of cup.

I was beamed up into a room
And it was designed as the moon,
Some aliens came in
And the biggest was the king.

The so called king
Had lots of rings
And opened his mouth,
Inside I saw a space mouse.

I screamed and screamed,
Then woke up from my dream,
But then I saw the king's tooth
And there was my proof.

Aimie Willemse (11)
Glashieburn Primary School

Dogs!

Dogs, big or small,
Pedigree or mutt,
I love them all,
I can't get enough of them at all.

Dogs, they are not a play thing,
Even though they cannot sing,
They play and play
And bark all day.

They're an individual,
Like us all,
They like to sleep,
In a warm bed
And that's my opinion about dogs.

Daniel Fenton (11)
Glashieburn Primary School

SEASONS

I like seasons, they are cool
Not winter, it's too cold,
In the garden, I want a pool
My dad will make it with his tools.

Springtime comes at last
Summertime soon yippee
In the harbour a lot of yachts,
All I can see is all their masts.

I do not like wintertime
It is much too cold
The only thing I like is to play in the snow
But then I found out my sledge was sold.

Autumn is really fun for me
I can climb the big bear trees
Yellow and green leaves fall down
Eventually they touch the ground.

That was some seasons I like
I love seasons - yes I do,
All year round they come and go
Some colourful and some dull.

Siobhan Wood (11)
Glashieburn Primary School

THE FUTURE

I can't wait till the future
It will be so much fun
You never know,
People might try to land on the sun!

There might be flying cars,
Different colours of stars,
New groups at gigs
And flying pigs!

I hope there might be robots,
Maybe dog, bird or cat,
Which would help out at home
And sleep on a many coloured mat!

Maybe every day travel will be to the moon,
We could use a space car,
Which I would name 'K A Boom!'
I can't wait till the future.

Anne Brown (11)
Glashieburn Primary School

DOGS

Dogs are my favourite pets
But I don't like it when they go to the vets,
Golden retrievers are the best,
They are better than the rest.

My grandma's dog is called Tess
When she was a puppy, she made a mess,
Caley and Megan are my auntie's dog's names,
Football and running are their favourite games.

I want a dog when I'm older
So I can put its picture in my folder
If I had a male, I would call it Rover
Then I would take it on holiday to Dover.

I think dogs are so much fun,
I like to play with them in the sun,
Not naughty or very scruffy
But cute and very fluffy.

Rebecca Thomson (11)
Glashieburn Primary School

My First Goal

It was the final of the cup
The score was two nothing to the opponents
Their team were on the attack
I stole the ball and started to run
The boy I stole it from thought it was a foul
But the referee said play on.

I had no one to pass to
So I went by myself
I dodged left and right
And ran past six different players
The boy I took down ran up behind me
My head hit the ground, he tripped me up.

The referee blew his whistle
It was a free kick just in our opponents half
I was told to take it as I was getting treatment
I stood up and put the ball in a position
I walked back ready to take it
I ran forward and kicked the ball.

The ball went high into the air
It was going wide
But then the wind took it
The keeper jumped and missed the ball
'Goal!' shouted everyone in the stands
We all started to cheer as we pulled one back.

The final whistle went five minutes later,
We were beaten,
But that doesn't matter,
We won runner-up
But I was happy because I scored my first goal!

Richard Morrison (11)
Glashieburn Primary School

THE WINNING GOAL

The ball came to my feet
And I took the ball and I started to run
Right at the opposition.
Dodging left, dodging right,
I dribbled through the defence
Until I was one on one with the keeper.

I was thinking if I should put it left
Or put it right or even chip it.
But just then I felt my whole body
Crash on the ground and the referee's whistle
Ringing in my ears and he points to the spot.

The referee took the ball and placed it on the spot
For me to take the penalty.
If I score this we are in the lead
But if I don't, we are not.
My nerves were really high and then the referee blew his whistle.

I ran up to the ball and I kicked it,
Hard enough to break a wall,
I watched the ball as it went into the net
A feeling of happiness swept over me.
We were in the lead!

The opposition kicked off and I was feeling great
That I had scored the leading goal.
But then the referee blew his whistle
And it was all over. We had won.
We were champions!

Logan Neave (11)
Glashieburn Primary School

MY BROTHER

When he throws a ball,
It goes right up in the air
And if I drop it, we don't really care,
When we eat sweets, we don't always share,
I wouldn't thump him, I wouldn't dare,
When we eat fruit, it is normally a pear,
If he got some biscuits, he would leave me a spare.

When tea is ready, he gets a call,
When he is outside playing football,
He doesn't play with an Action Man doll,
When he goes out, he goes to the mall
Because I am small, I think he is very tall,
Oh, I forgot, his name is Paul.

Mark Black (11)
Glashieburn Primary School

SEASONS

Spring

Here comes spring, hooray! Hooray!
Out come boys and girls to play,
Baby birds are hatching around,
There are no leaves piled over the ground.

Summer

The sun is so hot like never before,
Some children are playing along the shore,
The mums are so boring drinking tea,
While we are playing in the sea.

Autumn

Autumn is really fun for me,
For I can climb up a leafless tree,
Red and yellow hit the ground,
Falling right into a tiny mound.

Winter

In the winter falls the snow,
Making fields sparkle and glow,
Icy snowflakes hit off the ground,
Making it so hard to move around.

Andrea Willox (11)
Glashieburn Primary School

ELECTRONICS

Zooming right through cyber-space,
Come on let's have a race,
Right through cyber-space.

Playing on the Game Boy,
It's a great toy,
An electronic boat - ahoy!

A robot to help you with every day things,
It helps you with the doorbell 'ding'.
I'd like a robot to play the triangle 'ping'.

Mobile phones 'ring, ring' I've got my own,
I heard my mum groan,
When I got my mobile phone.

I have a PlayStation and it is fun,
There are lots of games, hear it hum.

Lauren McKenzie (11)
Glashieburn Primary School

SUPER SWIMMING

Today I'm going swimming,
I'm sure I'll have great fun
I hope my friends are going
Or I'll have to stay with Mum.

Now that we're here,
I'd dive into the pool,
If I do a belly-flop,
I would not look so cool.

Me and all my friends,
Swim underwater,
We have all had a good day
Acting like an otter.

Hayley Fletcher (11)
Glashieburn Primary School

FOOTBALL

Playing football is my game but
My best friend Logan isn't as good as me
Because he can't dodge the referee,
I've played in Cove Rangers stadium,
We got beat about 22-1.

I play in Champion Street with all my mates,
Into the final and out of the gates,
I loved every minute of the match
All the keeper did was go for the catch.

At the end of the day,
Maybe we might get some pay
Because of the work we put into train
I hope that we will make some gains.

Callum Maclean (11)
Glashieburn Primary School

A Time To Laugh

Happy children playing
Brightens everything around,
Laughing, singing, dancing,
It's a wonderful sound.

Grown-ups are so serious,
Not laughing like they should,
If only they could laugh and sing,
Instead of being rude.

Children are the best sunshine,
Include them in your day,
They will brighten up your life,
In a very special way.

Leeza Watt (11)
Glashieburn Primary School

ANIMALS

Butterflies have beautiful wings,
They fly about with birds that sing.
They're light as a feather
And feel nothing like leather.

I'd love to swim with dolphins,
But even better, I've held a falcon,
I really do like fish,
But not really when it's on a dish.

Dogs are one of my favourite pets,
But I don't like it when they go the vet.
Cats can nearly see in the dark,
But they really don't like it when dogs bark.

I have a horse named Sam
And he really doesn't like jam.
Horses are normally in the field,
But when it rains, they use a tree as a shield.

I love all kinds of animals
But even better I've ridden a camel,
I don't like it when they die
Because I always cry, cry, cry!

Lauren Reid (11)
Glashieburn Primary School

PEOPLE

The world is full of people,
Without people there is no world,
People are responsible for every action they make,
So don't be bad for your own sake.

People are given a body and they must take care of it,
People are given senses and they must use them,
We have legs and we walk with them,
Put your senses and your brain together,
Now we have a human being.

People rush,
Others tell you to hush,
We all try to
But sometimes we find it hard to shut our mouth!

We all have emotions,
We can cry and laugh by using our eyes and mouth,
We deal with things in our own way,
We go to school and learn how to work and
Communicate with other people.

Emma McLeman (11)
Glashieburn Primary School

MY PET CAT

My cat's name is Tia,
She is the best of them all,
But when she climbs trees,
I'm scared that she'll fall.

She sleeps all day and goes out all night,
Catching moths that come into sight,
She's a black, long haired cat
And she likes to sit on a mat.

She stays outside all day
But when she hears me rattle her mouse,
She comes inside to play.

Samantha Harris (11)
Glashieburn Primary School

PETS

Each rabbit has a bushy tail,
Even if they're male,
There are different breeds,
Who all like to feed,
Carrots are a bunny's best friend,
It makes them jump and bend.

Dogs have a good sense of smell,
They can always tell,
They need attention,
Not any neglecting,
They like to feed their face,
You've got to keep up the pace.

Cats sit and purr,
Or groom their fur,
They come in through their cat flap
And take a big long nap.

Hamsters store food in their pouches,
They then don't want to be touched,
They sleep in the day,
If you wake them up you'll pay.

Lisa Wilson (11)
Glashieburn Primary School

WINNING THE LOTTERY AGAIN!

Something amazing has happened to me,
My mum won the lottery!
17, 20, 12 and 10, 40 and 30, we've won again,
Those are the numbers that we used,
I couldn't believe it, we didn't loose,
It's the second time in 3 or 4 years,
Millions and millions and lots of tears,
We celebrated all night long,
The joy and laughter will never stop,
Fancy cars and fancy wine,
Partying all night, would be fine!
I live in a mansion, in the country,
With eighteen rooms and a pantry,
The hall's the size of a tennis court,
The rooms are big as well,
I'd never guess it would happen to me,
I think I'm doing well.

Nicola Smith (11)
Glashieburn Primary School

THE DRAW

There's only ten minutes to go,
A stunning match, here in Old Trafford,
Who will win, I do not know.

Man United take it up the wing,
As the crowds shout and sing,
The crowds stand on their seats,
Let's just hope that nobody cheats.

There's two minutes of extra time
And the goalie saves a shot on the line,
It's a throw in to Chelsea,
The rain is so heavy
So everybody is soaked.

Chelsea have got a penalty,
Against Man United's goalie,
The shot hit the right hand post,
Chelsea have got nothing to boast
And there goes the final whistle,
Chelsea now face Caledonian Thistle.

Fraser Gulline (11)
Glashieburn Primary School

GETTING READY FOR SCHOOL

I really enjoy school
Because Glashieburn is so cool.
I walk down roads and paths,
To get there in time for my maths.

I'm not to keen to get up in the morning,
I just stretch my arms and can't stop yawning,
My mum says nothing but gives me a glower,
Then I know it's time to get in the shower.

I come out of the shower as soon as I'm told,
Then I look out the window to see if it's cold,
The weather is poor, oh what a pain,
There's a howling gale and pouring with rain.

After that I get myself dressed,
I have my breakfast
And then I start being a pest,
Now it's time for school,
I better go!

Paula Malcolm (11)
Glashieburn Primary School

THE BIG MATCH

Today's the day we're going to win,
Watch you're not sent to the sin-bin,
We're going to beat the English team,
Yes, that would be a dream.

Come on, come on, it's about to start,
We're going to fight with all our heart.
The English truly are going down,
Walking off with a frown.

The game's kicked off, let's go for the ball,
It's very slippy so watch you don't fall,
Look out! England's on the break,
Come on give ourselves a shake.

No they've scored,
The crowd's getting bored,
Go on Jimmy you're on your own,
Well done, you've chipped the keeper,
It's a goal!

Ten minutes to go,
We've time to score,
Oh no Tom's down,
I can't take anymore.

It's down to me,
To tuck it away,
Right in the top corner,
It's made my day.

Paul Gray (11)
Glashieburn Primary School

BONGO BEAT

I'm in the jungle in the Safari heat,
Listening to the bongo beat,
The roar of lions,
The hiss of snakes,
Plenty of snaps I want to take.

Now I'm swinging with the monkeys
And hanging with the chimps,
Dancing with gibbons
And prancing to the beat.

The bears are eating,
The apes are roaring,
We're all cheering
To the bongo beat.

'Bongo, bongo in the kongo!'
They all sing with the bongo beat.

Katy Thomson (11)
Glashieburn Primary School

THE SWIMMING COMPETITION

I stand on the block,
I look at the water,
As firm as a rock,
I try not to hear the laughter.

I am still looking at the water,
I prepare now to go,
I throw myself high,
Twist, turn, land, low.

I cut through the water,
Like a fish I go,
No more jeering laughter,
I'm feeling high not low.

Greig Duncan (11)
Glashieburn Primary School

THROUGH THE ANTARCTIC

My trip to the Antarctic,
Was full of adventures,
I rode on the polar bears
And swam with the penguins.

I jumped over mountains,
I slept in an igloo,
I flew over white lands,
I love the Antarctic.

Something's beginning to shudder,
I'm feeling really scared,
Where do I go? What do I do?
No one can help me now!

The snow starts falling,
I can't even more
It's coming, it's falling,
I have to run!

I'm alive, I can hardly believe it,
The polar bears saved me
I jumped on their back
And rode to safety.

I'm home now
With a broken leg
But this was still
The best trip ever!

Claire Crawford (11)
Glashieburn Primary School

SPORT

Racing through on goal,
Coulthard's got the pole.
Serving on a big green court,
All this is to do with sport!

It keeps us fit,
We live for it.
Football, tennis, racing too,
These are played by people like you.

Football, football, it's the best,
It's simply better than the rest.
Raul, Rivaldo, they're both ace,
But who would win in a race?

Racing round the track,
The loser's fighting back,
They're near the end,
Just one more bend.

Craig Stephen (11)
Glashieburn Primary School

LUCKY NUMBERS HAVE DRAWN

My mum has won the lottery.
Hip, hip, hip hooray,
It's her lucky night tonight,
Here you must see the wonderful sight,
Everyone's dancing around.

Numbers drawn were 33, 6 and 2,
Let's invite the neighbours through,
The other three were 22, 16 and 43,
Now she'll spend more money on me.

She has money and relatives she never knew,
How come there are so many, phew,
Now she's throwing it all away,
Will it last another day?

I've decided what I want,
Lots of different toys.
Perhaps we'll maybe go on a jaunt,
At last our family are full of joys.

Lauren Gray (11)
Glashieburn Primary School

SCHOOL

I'm walking to school
I've got on my kagool,
Done my homework last night,
Before a spider gave me a fright.

Maths and language for today,
I'd rather stay at home and play,
Art tomorrow, I can't wait,
But if I don't hurry I'll be late.

Cross with the lollipop man,
Talk with friends about new boy Sam
Disco time tonight at eight,
Hope I find a Valentine date.

Alison Wylie (11)
Glashieburn Primary School

EVERYONE CAN DO SPORT

From tennis to polo,
From big teams to solo,
Everyone can do sport.

From swimming to boxing,
The smallest person coxing,
Everyone can do sport.

From those in their youth,
To those above fifty,
Even the ones who aren't quite so nifty,
Everyone can do sport.

From swimming pools,
To great big courts,
It's so much fun,
To play sports.

You can make new friends,
Have a good laugh,
Everyone can do it,
So why don't you have a shot.

Margaret Tough (11)
Glashieburn Primary School

THE FAST RIVER

Rushing through forests,
Dashing into lochs,
Shimmering in the sunlight,
Then it's out again.
Running down the River Dee,
Then straight to the sea.

Callum Stewart (11)
Maryculter West School

THE RIVER

Water gushes through the rushes,
Water splashes and it crashes,
The river rushes rapidly, while rippling,
The water's flowing and canoes are rowing,
The water splashes splendidly while steaming,
Water is blue, while currents pull you.

Paddy Rennie (9)
Maryculter West School

THE RIVER

Smash and splash,
The river plays,
Twisting and twirling through the mountain,
Slopping and slamming,
Against the rocks,
Sparkling and shimmering all the way,
Rapidly rushing to the waterfall,
Plunging down to the ground,
In the steamy spray,
Slipping and sliding,
All around
It eventually reaches the sea.

Leanne Bartlett (8)
Maryculter West School

THE RIVER

Starting in the ground, up it squirts,
Then beginning its journey down the hill,
Never stopping,
It begins to grow,
Faster and faster gathering pace,
It's now a national river,
There it goes,
Then begins to slow down as it nears the sea,
Twenty metres, then only one,
Now it's real life has just begun.

Allan Green (11)
Maryculter West School

THE RUSHING STREAM

Down the mountain goes the stream,
Splashing and playing as it goes,
Rushing and blasting like a rapid,
Going down the waterfall into the rocks,
It slams and crashes all the way,
All the way to the sea with the fish.

Martin Scott (8)
Maryculter West School

THE RIVER

The bubbling river flowed down and down,
It's going so fast that you would drown.
  Splishety, splashety,
  Splishety, splashety.

Splash! Splash! Down the waterfall,
There's people in a boat, oh no!
  Splishety, splashety,
  Splishety, splashety.

Someone at the edge pulls them into the bank,
But the boat falls down to the bottom with a clank.
  Splishety, splashety,
  Splishety, splashety.

The foamy bubbles look like acorns,
The hungry squirrel who'd been watching
Jumps away on all four paws.

Louisa Scott (10)
Maryculter West School

THE RIVER

Flowing through the mountain,
Rushed a small burn,
Twisting and turning, splashing and smashing,
Against the rocks,
Just a little further to the sea,
Down a steep valley shining in the sun.

Lizzie Green (8)
Maryculter West School

THE RIVER

The river starts its journey upon the mountain top
And trickles down the mountain it really mustn't stop,
Rushing round the twisty turns,
The rapid river runs,
Crashing, lashing and bashing in the shining sun,
Slowing down,
Running round,
The river mustn't stop,
Until it finds the sea,
Where it can be calm or not.

Martin Brand (9)
Maryculter West School

THE ARCTIC

In the Arctic lives the polar bear
You will also find musk ox there
There is the snowy owl
And the wolves that howl
There is the stoat
Which changes its coat
There is the seal
Which makes a good meal
For a polar bear
Who lives in the Arctic somewhere.

Ali MacLeod (9)
Maryculter West School

THE RIVER

The river splishes,
The river splashes,
The river crashes against the rocks,
The river lashes,
The river bashes,
The river rushes to the sea.

Fraser McTaggart (9)
Maryculter West School

A Cruel Spell

Tongue of dog, toe of frog,
Into the cauldron they go,
Bubble and broth,
Bugs in troth, put them in too,
Put in a snake, let it bake,
Let it pop, let it fill to the top.

Mhairi MacLeod (9)
Maryculter West School

SPLASH!

As the wave crashes against the rocks,
Twinkle on the water when it is smooth,
Plunging down,
The water flowing as walkers go past,
The water lashing,
Slamming against the land,
As the water comes down and down,
Faster and faster the water goes.

Steven Baxter (8)
Maryculter West School

THE RUSHING RIVER

The rushing river
Lashing and splashing
Round the rocks
Twinkling, gleaming
A blast of foam
And then a groan
Shining, shimmering,
Slowly swerving,
Round the reeds,
As it leads to the soothing sea,
Small burns trickle at my side,
I see ducks, swans, cars, people,
Fishermen, bridges and trees
As I slowly slide to the soothing sea,
I start to hear gulls calling,
I start to smell the smell of fish,
I near the sea,
I hear the waves,
I'm here at the soothing sea.

Jamie Bartlett (10)
Maryculter West School

THE LITTLE STREAM BELOW

Shining in the sun, the waterfall gushes,
Down to the little stream below,
Faster and faster,
Gathering pace,
Down through the mountainside,
Twisting and turning,
Down and down the water goes,
Until it reaches the little stream below.

Andrew Dingwall (11)
Maryculter West School

THE JOURNEY OF A VOLCANO

The magma is sizzling and bubbling,
Deep in the core, it tries to escape.

It finds a crack
And goes to attack.

It explodes with a thunderous rumble
And lava begins to tumble.

It cascades downwards.

Destroying everything in sight,
It gives the people a tremendous fright.

Its temperature is high
As the people start to cry.

It starts to cool down
As it covers the ground.

It slows to a stop,
Till the very last drop
And solidifies to rock.

Mark Cunningham (10)
Scotstown School

JOURNEY OF A VOLCANO

Burning, raging, boiling, oozing magma in the Earth's core,
We're in for trouble as molten rock forces its way up once more.
Rushing through the cracks and bursting through the layers,
The magma is much more vicious than a forest of angry bears.
The temperature is unbelievable, just below the Earth's crust.
When this volcano erupts the sky will be filled with clouds of dust.
Suddenly, a thunderous roar as a volcano billows out smoke.
The ash and gas is overcoming, its victims begin to choke.
Bursting out, the fluid lava cascades like a fountain,
Racing down the face of the raging, angry mountain.
Beware the dangerous destructive monster is now on the hunt,
Destroying, burning anything and anyone up front.

Deadly lava, deadly gas, deadly smoke and ash,
Fireballs are flying with the sound of
Whoosh and crash!

Slowly, the lava starts to cool, it is no longer hot.
This once angry monster solidifies, now it is solid rock.

Lisa Ponsonby (10)
Scotstown School

JOURNEY OF A VOLCANO

The magma starts its journey
Forcing its way up from the core,
The deadly hot lava erupts
Smoke fills the air and forms big puffy clouds.
The lava is oozing down the volcano
Making the surface look like a sheet of orange paper
When it is finished it leaves a deadly destruction.

Gregor Stewart (10)
Scotstown School

A Journey Of A Volcano

The core of the Earth is bubbling,
With magma sizzling up the cracks.
The molten rock travels to the surface
The volcano rumbles like thunder.
Then it erupts with great balls of fire
Shooting out like bullets from a gun,
The ground is covered in ash
Finally the volcano can rest again.

Kristofer Allan (10)
Scotstown School

THE JOURNEY OF A VOLCANO

A deadly volcano is lethal,
When it erupts the gases shoot up into the atmosphere,
And the smoke billows out in huge clouds
The lava thrusts its way into the air
And it cascades down like a fountain.
It flows like a river going at high speed,
Anything in its path will melt into nothing,
When the volcano stops it looks like the black sea
And bodies lie under ash forever.

David Gordon (10)
Scotstown School

THE JOURNEY OF A VOLCANO

In the core magma bubbles and splutters like a baby
When it finds a crack it surges to the crust.
Then it bursts through the crust with a thunderous roar.
It cascades like a bursting spot.
Lava runs down, like a swarm of blood-red cheetahs
Like blood devouring everything.
Then it all solidifies,
Grey lava lies in the sun peacefully.

Jamie Smith (10)
Scotstown School

JOURNEY OF A VOLCANO

The Earth's core bubbling and exploding
Magma is pushing upwards.
It will burst through the cracks to the surface,
The red hot lava rushes down the side of the mountain.
The puffs of smoke are shaped like a mushroom
All the ash is swept away by the wind.
The lava solidifies and changes the land
Craters are formed afterwards.

Stephanie Mitchell (10)
Scotstown School

JOURNEY OF A VOLCANO

Beginning at the centre of the Earth's core,
A big bubbling ball of fire.
It explodes its way to the Earth's crust,
Erupting into hot fiery lava and cascading down like a raging torrent.
The atmosphere is filled with clouds of thick, poisonous gas,
Lava rushes down the active volcano.
It's like a bully getting rid of anything in its path,
Ash and debris start to fly, as lava starts to solidify
Leaving behind a dead and burned land.

Louise Gray (10)
Scotstown School

Journey Of A Volcano

In the Earth's core there is exploding fire
It surges upwards to the Earth's crust,
Bursting out like a fountain with clouds of smoke.
Molten rock rains down like hailstones
Lava slivers down the volcano destroying everything.
A colourful orange and red river.
Silence is in the air as the volcano is fast asleep.

Lorna Dalgarno (10)
Scotstown School

A Journey Of A Volcano

Magma bursts out of the core,
It goes to the weakest point,
It powerfully bursts, looking awesome.
Fireballs fly out dangerously
Now it is active with deadly lava.
It is flowing down with powerful speed,
Like red-hot syrup oozing down,
The volcano is sleeping.

Rebecca Smith (10)
Scotstown School

THE JOURNEY OF A VOLCANO

Inside the Earth there is a core
Where there's molten rock, a hundred tonnes or more.
Then a crack forms on the Earth's crust,
And the magma is sure that it must
Burst out into the Earth's atmosphere
Causing panic, destruction and lots of fear.
Lava pours out everywhere,
No one would go near it, no one would dare.
It's so vicious, so awesome and hot,
There would be heaps of molten rock.
Many explosions are taking place,
The streams of lava seem to be having a race,
After a while the molten rock dries
It cools down and solidifies.
But there is still magma, burning the Earth's core,
Ready to start the journey once more.

Erin Grieve (10)
Scotstown School

JOURNEY OF A VOLCANO

Bubbling around in the core,
Starting a special volcano journey.
Looking for a weakness in the Earth,
Now the magma can escape.
It explodes upwards with smoke and fumes,
Then it cascades down the mountain
As the molten rock turns to lava,
It burns everything in its path.
Until it stops burning,
Which makes a new landscape.

Shaun Chapple (10)
Scotstown School

JOURNEY OF A VOLCANO

Molten rock bubbling inside the Earth's core
The magma rages upwards.
Zigzagging its way through and becoming
more powerful,
It's pushing its way out of the volcano.
Poisonous gas desperate to get out,
The explosive noise is deafening.
The lava cascades down the sides and piles up
and solidifies.
Making everything rock solid.

George Wetherly (10)
Scotstown School

THE JOURNEY OF A VOLCANO

A volcanoes journey is very long
A volcanoes force is rather strong.
A volcano inside, has lots of lava
It's probably hotter than a balaclava.
Seeing a volcano would make me stagger
Like I have drunk a lot of lager.
I have read about the Earth's core
Listening to it is such a bore.
People dying is so sad,
Volcanoes are sometimes bad.
I hope you enjoyed my little poem
Now I'd better be going.

Ben Jones (10)
Scotstown School

THE JOURNEY OF A VOLCANO

Fire inside the core is exploding
Finding a crack it surges up.
Shooting upwards rapidly with a thunderous roar
Cascading lava like a burning waterfall.
Oozing down the side like gloopy orange syrup,
Finished, it cools down and stops.
Silence is all around as lava solidifies and a
Crater is left.

Megan McKinnon (10)
Scotstown School

JOURNEY OF A VOLCANO

The Earth's core is full of bubbling magma
Molten rock is mighty and strong
It's waiting to burst and power its way through a crack
When the lava comes to the top of the volcano.
It is ready to thunder its way over the edge.
The raging, destructive lava running down the volcano side,
Smoke blinds your eyes.
The lava comes to a halt.
Then it reshapes the land.

Steven Sinclair (10)
Scotstown School

THE JOURNEY OF A VOLCANO

The volcano's journey began,
When it started to sizzle and bubble
As if it was in trouble.
The very hot lava got ready to flow.
Nothing could stop it so look out below.
It will cause destruction but then no one knew
That boiling hot lava will come out of the blue.
Covering everything in its way
The volcano erupted and got worse through the day.
This deadly volcano seemed in a hurry.
Smoke was in the air billowing like a cloud.
The lava cascaded down seeking things to bury.

There were many killed by ash and smoke,
So now we must somehow repair
The damage that was caused.

Charley Gavin (10)
Scotstown School

THE JOURNEY OF A VOLCANO

Magma runs through cracks that leads to the Earth,
It slithers through the cracks like a snake.
Eventually reaching the Earth's crust,
It cascades like a water fountain downwards.
Lava buries everything in its way.
Thick clouds of smoke fill the sky
When the molten rock cools down it hardens,
And the land is changed forever.

Deane Schembri (10)
Scotstown School

JOURNEY OF A VOLCANO

The Earth's core is made up of molten rock,
Which bubbles and rushes up to the crust.
Then the volcano is born
Once it reaches the surface it explodes,
And out bursts the hot lava.
Sending smoke and gas up into the atmosphere,
The lava flows like a river of water destroying
Everything in its path.
The houses are brought down to the ground,
Everything is destroyed.

Laura Bisset (10)
Scotstown School

THE JOURNEY OF A VOLCANO

The journey of a volcano
A large flaming ball is in the centre of the Earth.
When it manages to find a crack, it goes bursting up
It starts to climb up, getting hotter and hotter.
Fireballs can be very destructive,
Lava can destroy everything,
It shoots down the mountain.
Volcanoes knock down everything in its way.
It goes to sleep like a baby in its crib.

Mark Esson (10)
Scotstown School

Journey In The Dark

In my house I get up for a glass of water,
I see shadows.
My cuddly toys are like people, coming right at me.
I imagine pictures and posters are people,
I see all kinds of stuff.
I feel the monster want to grab me and take me away,
I drop my glass of water and soak my pyjamas.

Joanne Aiken (9)
Scotstown School

The Journey In The Dark

In the dark when I am in the car,
I see the cat's eyes at the side of the road,
I feel sleep, I hear the engine purring.
I see dark clouds that fill the sky,
the bright moon and the bright yellow stars.

Beckie Collie (8)
Scotstown School

GLASS OF WATER

I hear the floorboards creaking,
The wind blowing
I see my toys coming alive.
Coats turn into people
My dog comes closer, looking like
A monster.
I reach the kitchen, turn the tap on
Then go back to bed.
In the morning,
It's all over.

Michelle Wetherly (9)
Scotstown School

THE JOURNEY

I'm out camping in my dark spooky back garden
I think it's midnight
But I need a drink
So I get out my sleeping bag
Unzip the tent
I've got a key to the house
But as soon as I get out the tent
An owl's hoot makes me jump right out of my skin
The owl flies over the moon
Which looks like a huge UFO mother-ship watching,
Waiting to make its laser beam suck me up
I feel half scared, yet half excited.
I get in the house
Slam!
I trip over a skateboard
Fall right on my face
I scramble to the kitchen
Ding dong! Ding dong!
Ahh!
I jump out of my skin.
It was only the clock
When I get to the kitchen I jump
From outside I hear a dog howling like a wolf
I get my drink and go back out of the house
But I step on the cat's squeaky mouse
I run out to my tent
Zip it up
Get into my sleeping bag
I've had enough bumps in the night
I drift off to sleep.

Laura Sherriffs (9)
Scotstown School

THE JOURNEY

All the lights went out
I am slowly slipping into a dream
A boat waits on a cloud, gently for me
It floats through space and I'm
to catch stars
My net is heavy, the boat rocks from
side to side
A star is caught, it gleams with
blinding light
There is a zap, a tingling feeling runs
through my body
A groaning noise comes from somewhere
I wake up. It was Jemma snoring!

Lucy Kinnaird (8)
Scotstown School

THE JOURNEY

Journey to the toilet
Dad looks like a monster
wandering through the house.
Toys look like little creatures
of darkness.
Dad's snoring, sounds like a dragon
ready to blow fire.
My mind goes wild making everything
seem to come alive.
I need to get out of this world
of darkness.
When I switch the light on, it is all over.

Maxwell Robertson (9)
Scotstown School

JOURNEY IN THE DARK

Outside in the dark I see cat's eyes and street lights
I look and wonder what the shadows are
I hear the motion of the car and the engine
Yes! I'm going to the airport
I'm so excited, I can't sleep!

Kyle Donald (9)
Scotstown School

JOURNEY AT MIDNIGHT

I woke up
I looked at my watch, it was midnight
I had to get some water
I got up and out of my bed.
I missed my ladder, and my legs felt nothing
I fell about a metre
I hit the ground with a slam.
I got up and tiptoed to the hallway
I heard a creak
I froze, what was that?
I hid behind the coats
Phew! It's only my dad
I waited until he passed
Then I went into the kitchen.
I thought about it
I grabbed a tin of Diet Coke
And filled a glass.
I drank it all in one gulp
Then went out of the kitchen
Thro' the hallway
And into my bedroom
And up my ladder
Into my bed and snuggled up to my covers.

Stuart McDonald (9)
Scotstown School

THE JOURNEY

The toys are looking like something
I can't even imagine.
Clothes swerving like tornadoes
In the sky.
My dad is yelling like a monster
You can hear the clocks going
Tick-tock, tick-tock.
I'm tripping over the toys like
Blocks crushing together.
I hear myself going down the stairs
And the floorboards creaking.

Glen Rose (9)
Scotstown School

JOURNEY IN THE DARK

In my car I see shadows of fences shining on the road
Car headlights are like ghosts wailing past me
I see the cat's eyes on the road like monsters spying on me
A bus shelter is like a huge fire-breathing dragon watching me
Fiercely like it's going to pounce out at me
The planes are like shooting stars in the sky
I'm home now, the car sounds as if it's dying
When I get in my house I run up the stairs and
Up my stairs I see heads of statues
In my bedroom my TV looks like a huge eyeball
When I get into my bed I see all my posters like
People slyly drifting towards me.

Ben Jovanic (9)
Scotstown School

THE JOURNEY

In the dark inside I hear creaking floorboards
and sometimes I trip over toys on the floor.
I sometimes get a drink from downstairs,
then I see my dad, who looks like a monster.
In the dark I hear a clock ticking
and I see clothes like creatures.
I hear my own footsteps
and I see shadows of the toys.

Rahima Khatun (9)
Scotstown School

THE JOURNEY

I see my toys turning into monsters,
My clothes look like bats flying about in the wind
And my sister sleepwalking like a zombie.
I hear the wind howling like a wolf, the boiler clattering and
banging like a scary monster and the floorboards creaking.
I feel scared and frightened, as if I want to run back to my sleeping bag.

Joanne Davidson (8)
Scotstown School

Friday Night

Friday night I've just finished watching
The Mole. I put off the light and my
journey begins. I close the door with a creak.
It opens and I'm alone in the corridor,
the dark spooky corridor. The slimy floor
creaks so I run upstairs into my room.
At last I am safe in my room.

Andrew Ross (9)
Scotstown School

In The Journey

Inside my house at night
my toys look like they are away to come after me
and my clock ticking.
I see my brother sleep-walking
and he looks like a monster coming towards me
and glooming in my eyes.
I hear my own footsteps and
I hear my dad snoring.

Louise Morgan (9)
Scotstown School

THE JOURNEY IN THE DARK

I'm sitting in my car staring out of the window
I see trucks darting towards me like a herd of elephants.
I can see the cat's eyes, as if they're watching me
like I am under the spotlight.
I see the shadows of trees, the movements of animals
slowly turning into *mmmonsters!*
I see dull clouds coming out, the bright light moon
shining on the fields.
I hear the engine purring and the wind smashing and crashing
against the car window.
I feel the car rocking me to sleep.

Emma Turrell (9)
Scotstown School

THE JOURNEY

In the middle of the night I had
this dream about two green slimy
monsters with big red fierce eyes that
gleam in the light. The monsters are
edging towards me and I fall off
the cliff, but luckily there's a
submarine waiting for me. I climb in.
I go to a tropical island,
My mum switches the light on
and it's all over.

Bella Tabudravu (8)
Scotstown School

THE JOURNEY

I was out camping in Templars Park.
I turned to see the shadow of a massive slimy monster . . .
. . . but it was only the people in the next tent.
I got out of my sleeping bag, unzipped the tent
but I knew something was waiting to jump out at me.
A bat fluttered down and sat on my head,
I raced back to my tent, the others looked like dead bodies.
I zipped up the tent and hid in my sleeping bag.

Graham Walker (9)
Scotstown School

TIDAL

Tidal is like a big bath of water
It can get in a bit of a sotter
Sea crashing, banging against the rockpools
A bit like tools
Some animals, a bit like whales
Splashing with their tails
Children jumping over waves
With children hunting for a cave
Searching here and searching there
'Found it! Come here! Come here!'
Making sand castles
When mum's tie tassels
Underwater, the sea animals have a party
How many animals are there? Fifty!
The sea can be smelly
And rough
But I wonder what you think it's like?

Sarah Jane Scott
Stoneywood Primary School

BASKETBALL GAME

A ttempted to score a basket
B attered by the ball in the face
C runched by the biggest player on the court
D octor had to sort me out after the match
E mbarrassed for missing the shot
F lattened as the defender snatched the ball from me
G erbil ran across the court
H oisted the ball into the net
I ncluded a basket before half-time
J umping for the slam dunk
K eeping the ball away from the opponents
L arge opponent threatened me
M anager of our team seemed happy
N ods of happiness at winning
O ffence was good for our team
P enalty in the last minute
Q ualified for the next round
R an with ease up the court
S cored with a great shot
T alent of the other team was brilliant
U ttered to the other player on the court
V anilla ice cream van came round to sell
W alnut thrown through window to window
X ylophone started to play some music
Z oomed about in the last second.

Grant Rattray & Andrew Cook (10)
Stoneywood Primary School

WILD WILLIAM

Wazzup wild William
Walking wildly willingly
Watch out for that water William
Wap, splash, there goes wild William.

Hugh Florence (10)
Stoneywood Primary School

A Day At Blackpool Pleasure Beach

A   ttempted to go on the Pepsi Max
B   uying a big candyfloss
C   overed in sticky sweets
D   ying to go on all the rides
E   xcitedly waiting in line
F   inishing our candyfloss
G   rabbing Lynsey away from the sweets
H   anging on to our caps
I   gnoring the smell of the freshly baked doughnuts
J   umping happily as we are first in line
K   icking the ball in our favourite Arcade game
L   ooking for the best ride of all
M   aking the best of the day
N   oticing the Grand National in front of us
O   vertook the boy in the line
P   uking up on the rides
Q   uivering after coming off the Log Flume
R   ushing through all of the crowds
S   aying we won't regret going on the Pepsi Max
T   ipping upside down on the revolution
U   nbelievable the day is nearly up
V   omiting people on the rides
W   aiting in line to go to the toilet
X   exploring the rest of the park
Y   awning as the day goes by
Z   ooming to go on the last ride of the day.

Lynsey Robb (10)
Stoneywood Primary School

ELECTRICITY

E asy to switch on
L ight can be brilliant
E lectricity is energy
C urrent is very good
T rams can be using electricity
R egular electricity is the same as any others
I s the electricity on in your house?
C rammed into one house
I t can be renewable
T he electricity is all around you
Y ou have the electricity in your house

Adele Cormack (10)
Stoneywood Primary School

IF THERE WAS NO ENERGY

If there was no energy
No one would smell the sweet smell of the flowers
See the beautiful view from the hilltops
Walk in the greenery of the tree-filled forest
Or see the beauty of God's wonderful creations

No one would jump with joy on their birthday
Run through the grass with excitement
Go swimming in the bright blue sea
Or slide down the slide in the park

No one could rip open their presents at Christmas
Play an exciting game of football in the playground
Do their best at school so their mum would be proud
Or run and chase each other in the park

But there is energy
So yes, we can smell the sweet smell of the flowers
Yes, we can run through the grass with excitement
Yes, we can rip open our presents at Christmas
And yes, we can see God's wonderful creations.

Andrew Patterson (10)
Stoneywood Primary School

POLLUTION

Look around, what do you see,
Is it pollution or is it just me?
Ghastly rubbish everywhere,
Come on people, it just isn't fair.

Cars going round spilling out more,
Then washing the oily stuff into the shore.
The slimy black gold
Never gets old.

People dumping dreadful litter
And I feel very bitter.
If we could just take care of this space,
The world would be a better place.

Hayley McInnes (10)
Stoneywood Primary School

MY FAVOURITE MEMORY

Grandad always used to protect us
He always used to make us feel safe,
Grandad had skin as brown as the bark on a tree
He had hair as dark as the night sky.

Grandad had a watch with a face as large as the sun
He had ears as petite as buttons on a jacket.
Grandad had feet as gigantic as an elephant's trunk
He had a nose as long as Pinocchio.

Grandad had clothes as bright and dark as night and day
He had taste buds that would taste almost anything.
Those are the memories that will be in my mind all the time.

Siobham Robb (10)
Stoneywood Primary School

ENERGY

W ave power looks so calm and gentle
A t the seashore it smells of seaweed and the water smells of salt
V ery rough the sea can be
E verything is just so harmless

P ollution can be found in the crashing waves
O il makes the sea so glittery
W aves whooshing up the rocks
E xcitedly people swim in the sea
R unning through the rapid waves.

Liam Walker (10)
Stoneywood Primary School

REMEMBRANCE DAY

On the eleventh day of the eleventh month in 1920
'All men will go to war to fight for our country.'

All the men went to war that had to be chosen
I was chosen for the war in 1920
I was very scared to be shot
I have three children and a wife living in England.

We were so near to the beach
All you heard was bang, you could see the German soldiers
Shooting like mad trying to kill all their enemies.
I ran as fast as I could behind some bags full of sand.
I saw my friends being killed or blown to bits
Most people were taken prisoner.
On the eleventh day of the eleventh month
We had won the war
I couldn't believe it, I had survived.

So that is why we have Remembrance Day
On the eleventh day of the eleventh month.

Martin Kidd (10)
The Hamilton School

BACK TO SCHOOL

I've only been back to school two days
And I'm already feeling glum.
For I miss Cyprus and its nine hours of sun!
But now I'm home it's wind and rain
The thought of another twelve months of English
Is just driving me insane.

Mhairi Johnstone (10)
The Hamilton School

FIREWORKS

It was a cold and misty night
The chanting of the people was overwhelming
The smell of the hot dogs was amazing,
There was a countdown to the first firework
5,4,3,2,1. Lift-off!
The Catherine wheel was spinning as fast as it could.
The children were amazed and excited.
The night sky was lit up by a spectacular show;
Bang goes the rockets
Whizz goes the Catherine wheel
Pop goes the Squib.
The fireworks look like lovely flowers in the spring.
The sparklers went crackle
And the bangers went bang.
Then all of a sudden it went silent
The spectators were wondering what had happened
And then a huge bang!
Everybody clapped.
Some people were even crying.
There was a fantastic mood in the air.

Emma Jack (11)
The Hamilton School

FIREWORKS

The garden frosty cold
My father with the coal
There lined up in a row
The very smelly rocket show.
The orange glows of bonfires across the valley,
Fireworks go off, twisting like in a rally.
Everything stops and cats start to fight
But does the ghost of Guy Fawkes wander in the night?

Geoffrey Hodgson (9)
The Hamilton School

SILVER AND GOLD STARS

Silver and gold stars
Bejewel the night sky
When all of a sudden
Bang, crackle, pop.

Beautiful colours
Bejewel the night sky
And then they are gone
And we know we will
See them next year.

Charlotte Ross (11)
The Hamilton School

THE SNOW

Snow is there
Laying in the cold
Snow is all alone
No one to play with.

Children come out to play
But they can't stay out all day.
The snow is sad when everyone goes in
The snow is all alone again, in the cold.

Sleet is falling everywhere,
And the snow has got a friend.
Sleet is happy that he has a companion
Snow is dull as soon as sleet has gone.

Snow is happy when it gets friends,
Snow is a lovely thing.
Children like to play with it a lot
But kids are sad when it goes away.

Catherine Milne (11)
The Hamilton School

SNOW

Snow is like silver stars
Gliding in the sky,
It is like salt being sprinkled on chips
Snow is like crystals
Floating in the air.

Snow is as white
As a tidal wave
It is as cold
As an ice pole
Snow is as wonderful
As scoring a goal.

Snow is like polar bears
Dancing on the moon.
It is like a white cat
Lying on the ground.
Snow is like petals
Falling off a flower.

Snow is as cool
As a football.
It is as cold
As swimming in the North Sea.
Snow is as beautiful
As a mosque.

Snow is fun!

Grant Ritchie (10)
Tullos Primary School

FRIENDS

I have lots of friends -
Tall ones, small ones
Some boys, some girls,
My friends help me.
Sometimes they trick me
They are excellent friends

My friends come to my house
We chatter and play
My friends are cool
They're never cruel
They make me laugh and smile
They are splendid friends.

Steffi Aitken (10)
Walker Road Primary School

In My Head

In it there is a wild imagination
and ideas for everything
like getting cats that are up
a tree down.

There are job opportunities
which I shall consider
for a career.

An entirely new car
An entirely new dog
An entirely new boat.

A weird imagination

A good sense of humour

Me!

Wayne Stewart (10)
Walker Road Primary School

FIREWORKS

Sparkling, swirling in the air,
Colourful rockets everywhere,
It's an amazing glowing sight,
Lighting up the skies at night.
Rockets booming,
Swooshing, zooming,
Dazzling children big and small
Even the oldest of them all!

Daniel Hackett (10)
Walker Road Primary School

MICE

Mice, mice, they're so nice
I like to watch them skate on ice.
They run around but make no sound
On the cold and frosty ground.

Mice, mice, they're so nice
Their favourite food is cheesy rice,
In their cage they play all day,
Warm and happy there to stay.

Mice, mice, I love mice . . .
'Oh Mum! Please give me a mouse.'

Kirsty Adleigh (10)
Walker Road Primary School

DAD'S LONG LIE

Watching telly, playing sport
Marching soldiers to the fort.
Jumping, banging on the chair
If you rouse him, just beware.
In his bed, sleeping tight
Wake him up - he'll jump with fright!

Michael Milne (10)
Walker Road Primary School

INSIDE MY HEAD

In my head
I wonder
If aliens are true,
Or if animals can talk
Just the same as me and you?

In my head
I wonder
Will I ever be well-known?
Maybe make a film or two
Will my popularity have grown?

In my head
I wonder
If I'll end up very wealthy
But I know that I'll be happy
If my life is full and healthy.

Rachel Laing (10)
Walker Road Primary School

INSIDE MY HEAD

Inside my head there is the thought of flying to school in my bed,
Winning the lottery. Being rich.
Getting everything you wish.
Being in the Army driving a tank
Firing cannonballs at an old man's hat.
Being a famous football star
Having a big red fancy car.
Then I felt a breeze on my face.

I woke up in my flying bed
With a mountain of money and a crown on my head.
I was dressed like a football star
I even had my big red car.

I decided not to tell my mum
She really would not believe me.
I start to wonder if my dream
Is turning into reality.

Liam Harkins (10)
Walker Road Primary School

IN THE YEAR

January can be cold and dreary
Inside my house it's warm and cheery.

February brings St Valentine
Hope my true love remembers mine!

March is when I'm one year older
And my hair is pulled down to my shoulder

April's when I fool my friends
I hope their laughs will never end

May's weather is a wee bit warmer
I'm never cooped up in a corner

June is when school shuts its door
I can play outside for evermore!

July can be hot and sunny
When the beezzzz make lots of honey

August's when I'm back in class
How quick the summer seems to pass

September the trees wear autumn shade
And daylight colours begin to fade

October's when we're out at night
When all the neighbours get a fright

November's when fireworks soar above
It's a sight I really love

December's when choirs go carolling
Almost time for New Year to begin.

Jodie Dunbar (10)
Walker Road Primary School

My Mum

My mum is always on the phone,
Talking to her friends,
All the numbers she has phoned,
In a list that never ends.
If my mum stops calling people
That would just be great.
I could run and grab it,
Quickly, call a mate!
Will my mum ever come off the phone?
Well . . . that depends!

Gary Clark (10)
Walker Road Primary School

LOST

I've lost my way home,
I want someone to find me.
I'd travel the world
If someone would guide me
But no one is there.

Deep in the forest
I see a light.
I'll see if I can stay
Just for the night.
But no one is there.

Here is a house
I've seen it before
I know where I am
I open the door
My parents are there!

Lynn Duncan (11)
Walker Road Primary School

MY DOG

Carra is black and tanned
Carra licks my hand
Carra likes her food
Carra's never rude
Carra likes to play
Carra barks all day
I love my dog.

Michaela Kynoch (11)
Walker Road Primary School

FIREWORKS

It is fascinating in the dark,
When you see the flaming spark.
The shape of the fireworks is so grand
Catherine wheels spin above the land.
The rockets banging in the air
Delighting all the children there.

Natalie Pyper (10)
Walker Road Primary School

INSIDE A GIRL'S HEAD

In my head there is lots
I get up to things I should not do
I want to travel round the world
In a hot air balloon.
Portugal and Spain. Of course
You could come too.
I also want to stay in Florida,
For a day or two.
Will this dream come true?

Nadine Dargie (10)
Walker Road Primary School